W9-CPE-732

A Child's Garden of Yoga

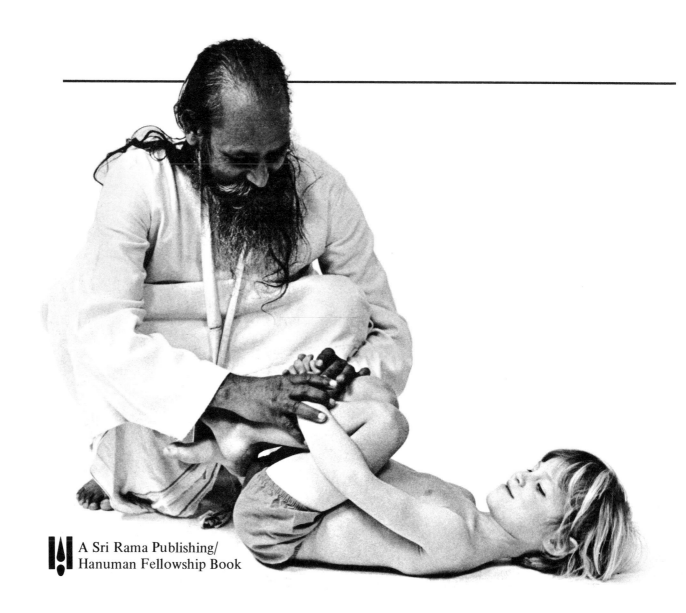

A Sri Rama Publishing/
Hanuman Fellowship Book

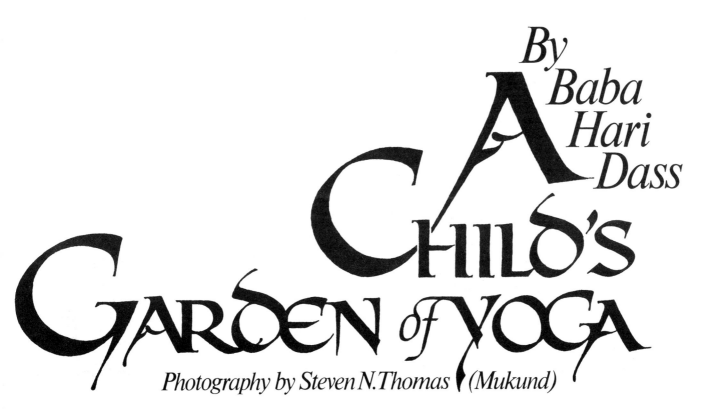

By
Baba
Hari
Dass

A CHILD'S GARDEN of YOGA

Photography by Steven N. Thomas (Mukund)

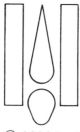 *Publishing Information*

© 1980 by Sri Rama Publishing

P.O. Box 2550, Santa Cruz, California 95063

Sri Rama Publishing is a non-profit organization
founded to produce the writings of Baba Hari Dass. Profits from the books
will go to support orphans in India or the United States.

Edited & typeset by Karuna Kristine Ault

Design, calligraphy, & production by Josh Gitomer

First printing: May, 1980

10 9 8 7 6 5 4

Library of Congress Catalog No. 80-80299   ISBN 0-918100-02-X

Contents

Teacher's Introduction

THE LIFE FORCE in the body *(prana)* is derived from the air we inhale. This life energy is the food of the mind. When sufficient life energy is produced through proper breathing, the mind grows stronger and sharper. Breath, life force, and the mind are connected. The main object of all Yoga practice is to unite the body, the breath, and the mind.

For children, Yoga is also a way of playing. Children from the ages of three to twelve years can do simple Yoga. These practices include the three basic locks *(bandhas),* deep breathing exercises *(pranayama),* meditation, and simple postures *(asanas).* These Yoga practices help to increase muscular coordination, maintain flexibility and good health, and calm the mind.

The digestive system of children is very strong; the intestines are so flexible that when some hard object is accidentally swallowed, it can pass through the intestines and come out through the stool. Yoga helps to maintain this kind of flexibility throughout the body.

For children it is difficult to control certain muscles, such as those used to press in the stomach, but with a little training in yogic methods they quickly learn to control and develop much of their muscular structure.

Breathing properly creates more life force to maintain a healthy body and strong mind. Improper breathing creates less life force, which results in poor health and an unsteady mind. By practicing deep breathing exercises (pranayama) children can learn to breathe fully and correctly. This allows more life force to energize the body, bringing physical health and mental well-being.

After energizing the body and mind through the practice of deep breathing exercises, meditation naturally follows. With proper training children can learn to sit quietly for meditation, and this will calm their minds.

The Five Centers

PRANA is the life force that energizes the entire universe. It is the energy of matter, the energy of mind, the energy by which all functions of the body are performed. Within the body, this life energy is concentrated in five centers.

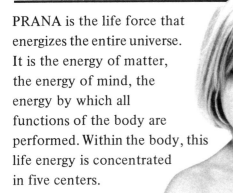

Throat Area: The energy in this center feeds and strengthens the mind. It moves from the throat to the top of the head. 1

Chest Area: The energy in this center draws vital forces from the air we breathe. The area from the nostrils to the chest is responsible for the function of breathing. 2

Navel Area: The energy in this center digests food and makes blood, sending nourishment to the whole body. 3

Pubic Area: Energy in this center spreads all through the body and helps in circulation. 4

Bottom of the Spine: The energy in this center pushes impurities out of the body through the urine and feces. 5

The Three Locks

BY PRACTICING the three locks (bandhas) the life
energy in the five centers is increased.

1 **Anal Lock:** Inhale gently and at the same time pull
the anal muscle up. Exhale slowly and relax the anal
muscle. Do this three times. This practice purifies the
energy and moves it upward to the navel area.

2 **Throat Lock:** Inhale gently and fill the chest with air.
Bend the head forward, trying to touch the chin to
the chest. Hold the breath for two or three seconds.
Lift your head and exhale slowly.
Do this three times. This practice
calms the energy and makes the body strong.

3 **Navel Lock:** Inhale gently. Then slowly
exhale while pulling the diaphragm up and
in. Hold for two or three seconds; then
relax and inhale slowly and gently. Do this
three times. This practice creates heat in the
abdominal area, which digests food and
burns impurities; this strengthens
the body.

Deep Breathing Exercises

We must learn to breathe properly. A good practice is to start the day with a few deep breaths in the open air. This opens up the lungs, allowing the body to receive more life energy (prana) all day long. It can also help us stay healthier.

1 Sit with a straight spine. Inhale gently and deeply through both nostrils, expanding the chest. Exhale gently. Do this five times.

2 Close the right nostril with the thumb of your right hand and inhale gently and deeply through the left nostril. Then lift your thumb off the right nostril, close the left nostril with the fingers of your right hand, and exhale gently through the right nostril. Do this five times.

3 Close the left nostril with the fingers of your right hand and inhale gently through the right nostril. Then lift your fingers, close the right nostril with your thumb, and exhale gently through the left nostril. Do this five times.

4 Inhale gently and deeply through the nostrils making the sound of a bee. Exhale gently, making the same kind of sound. Do this five times.

5 Extend the tongue and curl the sides so it looks like a pipe, or the beak of a crow. Inhale gently and deeply through this beak. Then pull the tongue in, close your mouth, and exhale gently through the nostrils. Do this five times. If you cannot roll your tongue, press it against the closed teeth and suck in air through the corners of the mouth. Then close your lips and exhale gently through the nostrils.

Meditation I

THE BEST TIME to sit for a short meditation is after practicing deep breathing exercises. Sit in a comfortable posture with your back, neck, and head in a straight line. Close your eyes and chant the sound of Om* in the following way: Inhale gently and deeply through the nostrils; then exhale singing the sound of "O", ending with the sound of "M". Do this Om sound five times (in five breaths).

---

* Om is the universal sound. It means all or everything. It is a Sanskrit word. Sanskrit is a very old language.

Now visualize a high mountain covered with forests and meadows. Feel the warm mountain earth under your bare feet. (Pause)

Visualize a vast ocean filled with waves. Watch the waves as they rise, fall, and rise again . . . . (Pause)

Visualize a flame of fire shooting straight up like a volcano. Watch the bright colors of the fire as it grows higher and higher, and feel its heat. (Pause)

Visualize a strong wind whistling through trees. As it passes by, it blows leaves, grass, and dirt into the air. (Pause)

Visualize a clear blue sky. There is no wind, no sound. All is perfectly still. It is so calm that you can hear the sound of your heart beating. (Pause)

Now chant Om once. Open your eyes. Stretch your arms and legs. Draw a picture of your meditation.

SIT WITH HEAD, neck, and back straight and picture the following story in your mind.

Once you wanted to know what was behind the sky. So you went out in search of it . . . .

You are walking on the meadows where there is green grass and where yellow and blue flowers grow. The birds are singing. Now you are walking in the grass. Look! The grasshoppers are hopping away when they see you coming.

Oh, it's a beautiful meadow. What's that over there? Looks like a hill. Let's go there. Climb up to the top of the hill. Now you can see everywhere. There are jungles with tall trees on one side, and on the other side are houses and roads. This is all on the same Earth.

Far, far away there are no trees, no towns. It looks like the sky is touching the earth. Let's go there. Oh, it's an ocean. Look, the waves are rolling one after another. Some crash on the beach, and some are hitting and pushing each other, making noise all the time. You can see seals sitting on the rocks. Hear them barking? You can see fish in the waves, and close to the beach you can see crabs and frogs. Gulls are swooping overhead. Their shrill cries pierce the air.

Let's go to the jungle. It's now summertime. There is no rain. The grass, bushes, and trees are all dried up. Look! there's a fire. How fast it is burning the bushes and trees! Look at the flames rising high up in the sky. Hear it crackling. Oh, the fire has scared the deer. They are running away. Can you hear their feet pounding the earth? The fire is spreading everywhere. Let's go away.

Meditation II

Now you are standing in a desert. There are no trees, no grass, no water. Everything looks dry. Oh, what is this? It's a whirling wind. Anything that comes in the path of that whirling wind goes round and round and rises up in the sky. Oh, *you* are in the whirling wind. You are going up and up in the sky. Do you see the sky all around you? There is nothing. You are still going up and up, and still there is nothing. Oh, look, that's a cloud coming close to you. The cloud is making you cold and wet. Go above the cloud. Now you are floating high up in the sky. There is nothing. No clouds, no birds, no sound, just complete silence. But still you see the blue sky. It is endless. Let's go back. You are sitting with your eyes closed. Chant Om, and open them.

Introduction to the Asanas

THOUSANDS OF YEARS ago people were practicing Yoga in jungles. They would watch other people, trees, animals, birds, snakes, fish, and insects very carefully, and they began to imitate with their bodies some of the things they saw in creation. They noticed that when an animal became sad or sick, it would sit or stand in a different position, and the new position would help cure the illness. So they understood that body postures are helpful in curing diseases and maintaining good health.

In this way the ancient yogis designed the system of asanas to keep the body strong and flexible, to exercise the internal organs and glands, and to tone the nervous system. Asanas also improve circulation and relax the body and the mind.

And asanas are great fun, too!

Before you begin the practice of asana, it is important to become familiar with the following rules:

1. Practice before eating, or wait for three hours after a meal. If you are hungry, you can drink a glass of milk before practicing. After asanas, wait twenty minutes before eating.

2. Choose a quiet, well-ventilated place free from wind, smoke, or dust.

3. Wear light, comfortable clothing.

4. Lie on a blanket or pad to protect the body from cold and bruising.

5. Do a few warm-up exercises before practicing asanas. Warm-ups can be done to music. Hop up and down for a few minutes to warm your body. Do a few sit-ups to loosen the legs. Then practice the following exercise for the spine: Lie down on your back and cross your legs; hold your feet with your hands and roll back and forth on the spine.

6. Breath should be normal when doing asanas.

7. After doing three or four asanas, do the Rest Pose for ten to twenty seconds; then continue with other asanas.

8. Upon finishing asanas do the Rest Pose for ten to fifteen minutes; relax the mind and body.

9. Do your best without straining the body. Don't get discouraged if you can't do what others do. Practice every day for perfection.

Let's warm up!

Hop a few times; first on one foot, then. on the
other, then on both feet.

ASANAS
for Children from the Ages of Three to Six

Palm Tree

Stand with your feet together, arms at your sides.
Lift your right arm high above your head. Rise up
on your toes, and at the same time stretch your
left arm down. Hold for three seconds; imagine
that you are a giant palm tree. Now raise your
other arm and repeat the asana; then try with both
arms above your head. Try to reach high into the sky.

Flat on the Floor

Bend down and touch the floor with
your hands. Can you put your palms flat on
the floor without bending the knees?

Sit down and stretch your legs
straight out in front, feet
together. Touch your toes with
both hands. Don't bend your knees.
Can your head touch your knees?

Touch
Your Toes

Ride Your Bike

A. Lie down on your back. Lift your legs
off the floor. Can you rotate your legs in a circle as if
you are riding a bicycle? B. Now rotate both hands
and feet in circles and laugh loudly. Hey, what's so funny?

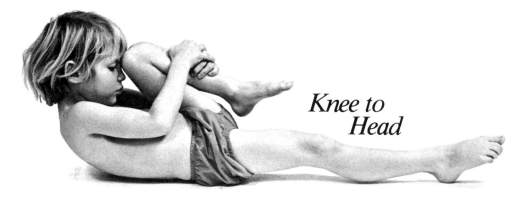

Knee to Head

Still lying on your back, bend the right knee
up to your chest. Wrap your arms around the
leg and pull it toward your chest. Now bring
your forehead up to touch your knee. Hold
this position for three seconds; then release.
Raise your left leg and repeat the pose. Then
raise both legs together and repeat the pose.

Sparrow

Squat down with feet
apart, shoulders and arms on
inside of knees. Bring your
arms under, behind, and around
your legs. Touch your toes
with your hands. Look up. This is the
Sparrow Pose. Can you hop?

Sit down and stretch both legs straight
out in front. Hold your left toes
with the left hand. Grab your right foot with the right hand and try
to pull it back to your right ear. Keep your left leg
straight; don't bend the left knee. Now
switch legs and pull the left leg to your left ear. You can
also try to cross your legs and pull the top leg
up to the opposite ear; that is,
right toe to left ear, left
toe to right ear.

Bow & Arrow

Half Locust

Lie down on your stomach, arms at your sides with palms on the floor. Raise your right leg off the floor. Lower it, and then raise the left leg. Next try lifting both legs together, pressing down on the floor with your arms. This is the Half Locust Pose. Lower your legs and relax.

Bow

A. Bend your legs and lift your feet off the floor. Reach back and grab your feet or ankles with your hands and hold your legs close to you. Look up.

B. Now pull on your feet, lifting your knees off the floor, and stretch like a bow. Come down slowly, let your legs back down and then relax.

Cat

Put your hands on the floor in front of you and stand on "all fours" like a cat. Now lower your head and stretch your back up, breathing in slowly through your mouth. Then exhale slowly while raising your head and sinking your back down into a deep curve. Look up. Do this several times.

Cobra

A. Keep your palms and forearms on the floor, and lift
your head and chest. Stretch your neck up and back. Look up.
Come down slowly.

B. Now place your palms on the floor beside your shoulders.
Push your head and chest up like a cobra. Look up. Come
down slowly.

Thunderbolt

Come to a kneeling position and sit on your heels. Put your hands on your knees and take a few deep breaths.

Pine Tree

Stand up and balance on your left leg; bend your right leg and place the right foot on the left thigh. With palms together, fingers pointing upward, raise your arms over your head. Balance in this pose and imagine you are a tall tree. Stand on the right leg and repeat the pose.

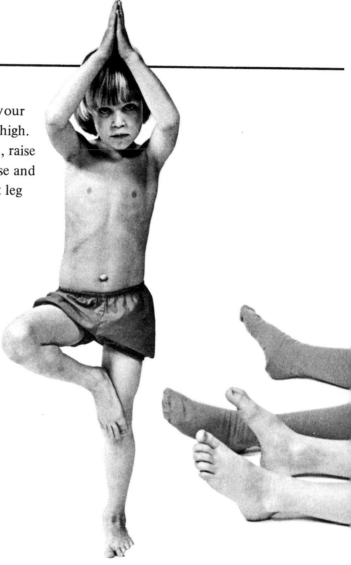

. . . and Rest

Lie down on your back, arms at your sides. Feet
should be a little apart, head rolled to
one side. This is the Rest
Pose. Now close your eyes
and relax. (See *Deep
Relaxation,* page 104.)

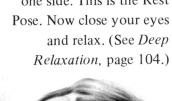
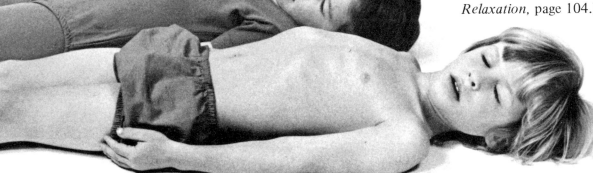

ASANAS
for Children from the Ages of Six to Twelve

Salute to the Sun   1   2   3

1. *Salutation Pose*
Stand straight with your feet together. Put your palms together and hold them in front of your heart, fingers pointing upward.

2. *Upward Salutation Pose*
Stretch your arms up over your head and bend back as far as you can.

3. *Hands to Feet Pose*
Bend forward and place hands on the floor beside the feet. Keep your legs straight and try to touch your knees with your forehead.

4. *One Foot Extended Pose*
Keeping palms flat on the floor, stretch your left leg straight back and bend your right knee in front of your chest. Left knee rests on the floor. Look up.

5. *Both Feet Extended Pose*
Bring the right leg back to meet the left. Only hands and feet touch the floor; head, back, and legs should form a straight line.

4   5

6. *Eight Limbs Bowing Pose*
Lower the body and touch knees, chest, and forehead to the floor.

7. *Snake Pose*
Raise the head and chest off the floor by straightening the arms. Bend your head back, keeping shoulders raised. Look up.

8. *Mountain Pose*
Raise your buttocks, keeping arms and legs straight. Head is down; try to touch your heels to the floor. The body looks like an upside-down "V", a mountain.

9. *One Foot Extended Pose*
Bring your left foot forward between your hands, keeping right leg stretched back. Look up.

10. *Hands to Feet Pose*
Bring your right foot up to meet the left. Make your legs straight and try to touch your forehead to the knees.

6   7

8

9

10

11

12

11. *Upward Salutation Pose*
Raise your arms up over your head and bend back as far as you can.

12. *Salutation Pose*
Lower arms and put your palms together in front of your heart as in the first position.

Shoulderstand Pose

Lie down on the back with arms at your sides. Slowly raise legs straight up. Now lift your hips and back off the floor, and try to straighten your whole body so it points up toward the sky. You can support the back with your hands and balance.

Ear-Knee Pose

From the Shoulderstand slowly lower the feet down over your head until your toes touch the floor. Bend legs and bring knees down to your ears. Keep arms flat on the floor behind your back. When you are ready, roll out of this pose until you are again lying down on your back. Rest for a minute.

Fish Pose

Lie on your back, legs together. Arch your
back and rest the top of the head on the floor. Put
your palms together over your chest; imagine that your
arms are fins. Hold this pose for three to
ten seconds; then release and
slowly lie down again.

Leg Lifting Pose

Lie on your back, legs together. Keep your arms at your
sides with palms facing down. Slowly raise your right leg
as high as you can without bending your
knees. Hold for five seconds; then lower
it slowly. Repeat this pose with the
left leg, then with both legs together.
Be sure to keep your back, neck and
head on the floor.

Lie on your back. Raise your legs and hips into the air.
Lower feet toward the floor over your head. Keeping
arms straight, place palms on knees to support
your legs. Balance in this pose for five seconds;
then slowly lower your legs to starting
position.

Tranquility Pose

Wind-Releasing Pose

Lie on your back, feet together. Bend
the left knee up to the chest, pulling it tight with
hands clasped around it. Bring your forehead
up to touch the knee, keeping right leg straight. Hold this
pose for three seconds; then lower leg.
Repeat with right leg bent, then with
both legs together.

Back Stretching Pose Lie on your back, feet together, with your arms stretched over your head. Rise up to a sitting position; then bend forward and grab your toes. Try to touch your forehead to your knees. Hold this pose for three seconds; then slowly rise up to a sitting position and lie back down on the floor.

Lie on your back. Grab feet with hands and pull them toward your forehead. Raise your head and touch toes to forehead if you can. Hold for three seconds; then release feet and slowly lower legs.

Baby in the Womb Pose

*Turtle
on the Back*

Lie on your back. Raise legs up and over your head with feet apart. Put arms between legs over the backs of your knees. Press your toes, knees, and palms to the floor. Hold for three seconds; then slowly release legs and lower them.

Rest Pose

Lie flat on your back, arms at sides and head
rolled a little to one side. Close your eyes
and relax your whole body.
Note: Do the Rest Pose for ten to twenty seconds
after every three or four asanas. Do the Rest Pose
at the end of your asana practice for at least five minutes.

Half Locust Pose

Lie on your stomach with your chin resting on the floor. Put your hands under your thighs with palms down. Slowly lift the right leg as far off the floor as possible without bending the knee. Hold the pose for three seconds. Then slowly lower right leg and repeat with left leg. Now raise both legs together in the same way.

Alligator Pose

Lie on your stomach, feet together and arms at sides. Raise your head, shoulders, arms, and chest off the floor. Look up. Hold this pose for three seconds; then come down slowly.

Full Alligator Pose

Lie on your stomach, feet together and arms at sides. Raise head, shoulders, arms, and legs off the floor. Look up. Hold this pose for three seconds; then slowly lower body and relax.

Bow Pose

Lie on your stomach. Bend your knees and reach back to grab ankles with hands. Now pull on your feet, raising knees, thighs, head, and chest off the floor. Stretch your body like a bow. Look up. Hold this pose for three seconds; then slowly lower body and relax.

Cobra Pose

Lie on your stomach, feet together. Place your palms on the floor beside your shoulders. Raise head and chest off the floor as far as you can; look up and back. Hold this pose for three seconds; then come down slowly and relax.

Grasshopper Pose

Lie on your stomach. Keeping knees together on the floor, bend lower legs up toward head. Place hands on your back at the waist, lift your head and chest off the floor, and look up. Hold this pose for three seconds; then slowly lower your body to the floor.

Reverse Rest Pose

Lie on your stomach, feet apart, palms facing down.
Turn your head to one side. Close the eyes and relax
the whole body.
Note: Do this pose for ten to twenty seconds after
every three or four asanas done on the stomach.

Stretched Bow Poses

A. Sit with legs straight out in front. Cross your feet, putting right ankle over left ankle. Bend forward and grab your feet, without crossing your arms. (Left hand grabs right foot; right hand grabs left foot.) Now pull right foot (the one on top) with your left hand, bringing it up to your left ear. Keep your left leg straight. Hold this pose for three seconds; then reverse legs and repeat.

B. Sit with legs straight out in front. Bend forward and grab your feet with your hands. (Right hand to right foot; left hand to left foot.) Now pull your left foot up to your left ear. Hold for three seconds. Straighten left leg and pull right foot up to right ear in the same way.

Seagull Pose

Sit on your left heel and
stretch your right leg
straight back. Spread your
arms out to either side
and bend back as far as
you can. Switch legs
and repeat.

Nobility Pose

Sit on the floor. Bring the soles of the feet together
and clasp your hands around your feet. Pull your heels in
as close to your body as you can, and try to press
your knees down to the floor. Sit up straight.
Hold this pose for three seconds.

Star Pose

Sit on the floor. Put the soles of the feet together and pull them close to your body. Raise your knees to about as high as your chest. Cross your fingers and put your hands on the back of your neck. Bend forward, rest your head on your feet, and put your elbows on the floor. This makes a five-pointed star: two elbows, two knees, and the top of the back.

Bowing Pose

Sit on the floor. Bring the soles of the feet together in front of you and keep them away from the body so the legs form a square. Hold your feet with your hands and bend forward until your head touches the floor behind your heels. Hold this pose for three seconds.

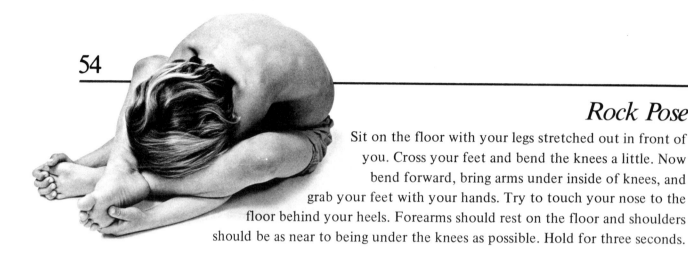

Rock Pose

Sit on the floor with your legs stretched out in front of you. Cross your feet and bend the knees a little. Now bend forward, bring arms under inside of knees, and grab your feet with your hands. Try to touch your nose to the floor behind your heels. Forearms should rest on the floor and shoulders should be as near to being under the knees as possible. Hold for three seconds.

Bat Pose

Sit on the floor. Bring the soles of the feet together in front of you. Raise your knees. Now lean forward and slip arms under inside of knees, palms down. Extend your arms straight out to the sides until backs of knees rest on shoulders. Chin rests on floor behind heels, or on the feet. Look up as much as possible. Hold this pose for three seconds; then come up slowly.

Half Spinal Twist

Sit on the floor with your knees raised. Let your
left knee drop to the floor as you pull your left
foot under raised right knee. Place left foot beside
right buttock. Now cross your right foot over
folded left leg and place it flat on the floor on the
outside of your left thigh. Twist your head to the
right, cross your left arm over your right thigh,
grab your left knee with left hand. Put right
arm behind your back, looking back over
right shoulder as far as possible. Hold
this pose for three seconds; then
reverse legs and repeat.

Cow's Head Pose

Sit on your heels; then shift the buttocks to the left and sit on the floor beside your heels. Now raise your right knee, pull your right foot over folded left leg, and place it alongside your left thigh. Raise your right arm over right shoulder and bend it so the hand hangs down your back. Put your left arm behind your back and bend it so the hand reaches up toward your other hand. Now join your hands and stretch. Hold this pose for three seconds; then slowly release. Reverse legs and arms, and repeat.

Thunderbolt Pose

Sit on your heels with the knees together. Put
your hands on your knees. Keep your back,
neck, and head in a straight line. You may sit in this
pose for several minutes.
Note: The Thunderbolt Pose can also be
used as a meditation pose.

Cricket Pose

Sit on your heels, knees together. Lean forward and put
your forearms and palms on the floor beside your knees. Rest
your chest on your knees, raise your head, and look up.

Pigeon Pose

Sit on your heels, knees slightly apart. Lean
forward, lifting the buttocks off the heels.
Then reach back between your legs and
grab your heels. Stretch your head and neck
upward. Look up. Hold this pose
for three seconds.

Deer Pose

Sit on your heels, knees together. In one
movement, swing arms back and up and raise your
buttocks off your heels. Stretch arms straight
back; bend your wrists and stretch your fingers upward
like antlers. Head is up; look straight ahead.

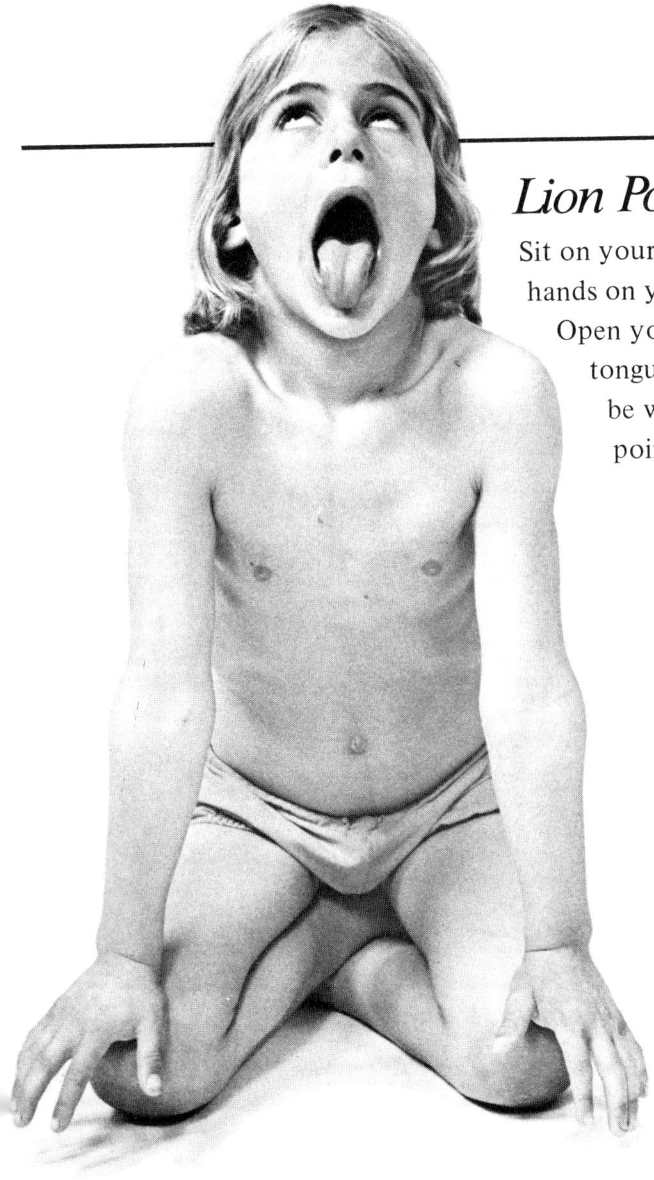

Lion Pose

Sit on your crossed heels with your knees apart. Put your hands on your knees and stretch the fingers wide apart. Open your mouth as wide as you can and stretch your tongue out and down as far as possible. Eyes should be wide open, rolled upward and focused at the point between the eyebrows.

Camel Pose

Sit on your heels, knees slightly apart. Reach back and grab
your heels with your hands. Now raise the buttocks up and
forward, arching your back and bending your head as far
back as you can. Your arms should be straight. Hold the
Pose for three seconds; then come down slowly and relax.

Tortoise Pose

Kneel on the floor, feet slightly apart; then sit on
the floor between your feet. Spread your
knees apart. Now stretch forward and
touch your palms, arms, chin, and
chest to the floor. Buttocks should
stay on the floor. Hold
this pose for three
seconds; then
come up slowly.

Boulder Pose

Kneel on the floor. Lean forward and put your head on the floor in front of your knees. Lift your feet off the floor. Grab your lower legs with your hands and pull them in toward your body. Balance for three seconds; then come up slowly.

Baby Pose

Sit on your heels with arms at your sides. Lean forward and touch your forehead to the floor. Arms stretch back toward feet, palms up, resting alongside your legs. Make your body as small as possible. Hold this pose for thirty seconds; then come up slowly.

Cat Pose

Kneel on the floor on "all fours". Breathe in through your mouth with a hissing sound. At the same time, arch your back up like an angry cat, bringing your chin into your neck. Then exhale through your mouth while raising your head up and sinking your back down into a deep curve. Look up. Do this 4 times.

Palm Tree Pose

Stand with feet together, arms at your sides. With a swinging motion, raise your right arm high over your head. At the same time come up onto your toes and stretch your left arm down. Hold for three seconds; then come down and repeat pose with left arm raised. Now try raising both arms. Imagine you are a tall palm tree.

Tree Pose

Stand with feet together. Put the sole of your left foot on the inside of your right leg, as high as you can. Arms go above your head with palms together, fingers pointing upward. Balance for three seconds; then reverse legs and repeat.

Eagle Pose

Stand with feet together. Cross your left thigh over your right thigh, hooking your left foot behind your right calf. Then cross your arms at the elbows and wrap lower arms around each other. Place palms together, fingers pointing upward. Now bend your knees and try to touch the ground with the left toes, like a roosting eagle. Reverse legs and arms and repeat.

Half Moon Pose

Stand with your hands on your hips or on your buttocks. Bend back as far as you can without straining, keeping your legs straight. Hold the pose for three seconds; then come up slowly and relax.

Angular Pose

Stand with feet apart, arms outstretched to either side. Twist upper body to the left, bending forward, and touch your right hand to your left foot. Try to look at your left hand; it is stretched straight up. Hold this pose for three seconds, come up, and repeat on the other side.

Ghost Pose

Stand with feet apart. Bend forward,
bringing your head, shoulders, and arms
behind your legs. Now either grab
your heels with your hands, or
bring arms behind knees and
clasp hands behind back.

Sparrow Pose

Squat down with feet apart,
shoulders and arms between
knees. Bring your arms behind
your calves and place your
hands on top of your feet. Look
up. Now lift your heels off the floor,
balancing on your toes; then
come down. Do this several
times.

Squat Pose

Stand with arms at sides,
feet apart. Bend your knees
and squat down, balancing
on the balls of your feet.
Place hands on waist or on
knees. Look straight ahead.
Slowly come back up to standing
position.

Triangular Pose

Stand with your feet wide apart.
Slowly sit down, touching your knees
and buttocks to the floor. Your legs
should be bent at right angles,
with knees together and facing
each other. Place hands on
knees and look straight
ahead. Slowly stand up.

Flower Pose

Sit on the floor with your knees bent. Slip your arms under your knees and raise your feet off the floor. Open your hands and point your feet upward. You are a blooming flower. Hold for three seconds and release.

Dwarf Pose

Kneel on the floor. Lift your feet off the floor and grab them with your hands. Now walk on your knees, looking straight ahead. Try to hold still and balance on your knees. Slowly release your feet.

Monkey Pose

Squat down with your feet apart.
Bring your arms between your legs and press your buttocks with
your hands. Look up and lift your heels off the floor. Hold
this pose for three seconds; then come down.

Duck Pose

Squat down on your toes with palms on the floor in front of your legs. Lean forward and raise your body and feet off the floor, resting your knees on your upper arms. Hold this pose for three seconds; then come down slowly and relax.

Lotus Pose

Sit on the floor with your legs crossed. Put the left foot on top of the right thigh; then put the right foot on top of the left thigh. Place your hands on your knees. Keep your head and back straight.

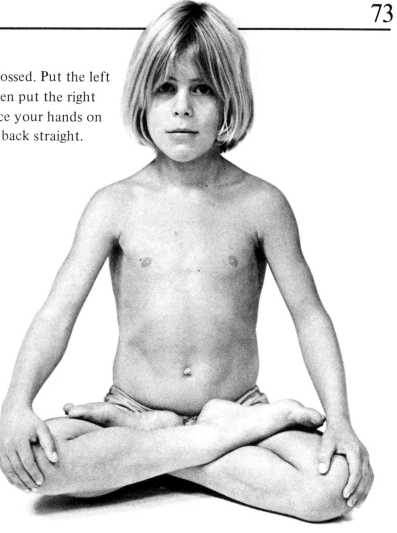

Sit in the Lotus Pose. Then cross your arms
behind your back and grab your big
toes with your hands.

Bull Pose

Sit on the floor and pull your right
heel to the inside of your left
thigh. Bend your left leg back
so that the left heel rests
beside your left hip. Place
your hands on your
knees.

Bound Lotus

Easy Pose

Sit with legs crossed. Keep your back straight,
hands on your knees. Close
your eyes.

ASANAS *For Fun!*

For the following asanas, you will need a group of at least eight children. The asanas are done in a circle; they form patterns like wheels, snowflakes, or the petals of a flower.

77

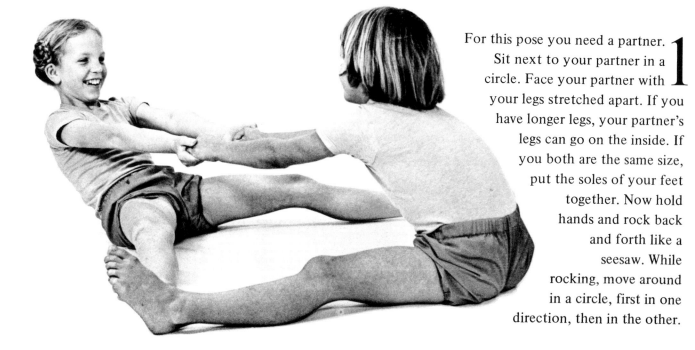

For this pose you need a partner. 1
Sit next to your partner in a
circle. Face your partner with
your legs stretched apart. If you
have longer legs, your partner's
legs can go on the inside. If
you both are the same size,
put the soles of your feet
together. Now hold
hands and rock back
and forth like a
seesaw. While
rocking, move around
in a circle, first in one
direction, then in the other.

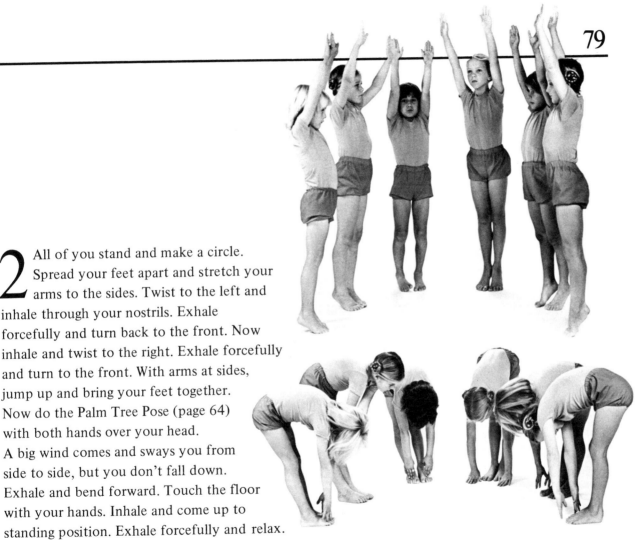

2 All of you stand and make a circle. Spread your feet apart and stretch your arms to the sides. Twist to the left and inhale through your nostrils. Exhale forcefully and turn back to the front. Now inhale and twist to the right. Exhale forcefully and turn to the front. With arms at sides, jump up and bring your feet together. Now do the Palm Tree Pose (page 64) with both hands over your head. A big wind comes and sways you from side to side, but you don't fall down. Exhale and bend forward. Touch the floor with your hands. Inhale and come up to standing position. Exhale forcefully and relax.

3 Stand and make a circle. Hop and spread your arms and legs apart (Starfish Pose). Hop and bring them back together (Stick Pose). Clap your hands on your sides. Hop and bring left arm and left foot back, right arm and right foot forward (Soldier Pose). Hop again and bring arms and feet back together and clap (Stick Pose). You are now facing ¼-turn to the left. Repeat the whole sequence—Starfish, Stick, Soldier, Stick—four times until all are facing the center again. You can do it fast and count by naming the poses. At the end do Stick Pose and Hop! Hop! Hop!

4 Do the Tree Pose (page 64); then hop. Now clap your hands—be a clapping, hopping tree. Now be an eagle (page 65). Pretend you are perched on top of a tree, surveying the land for miles around. Can you jump?

5 Make a circle. Sit on the floor with your knees raised. Hold hands. Lift your arms and bend back as far as you can without lying down. Then come up. Now straighten your legs. Hold hands. Raise your arms and lean back until you are lying down. Slowly lift your right leg straight up, keeping it at a right angle to your body. Lower right leg, then do the same with your left leg. Lower left leg, then lift both legs together. Don't bend the knees. Now slowly lower your legs. Lift your legs again and rotate them as if riding a bicycle. (See page 19.) Go faster. Laugh—Ha! Ha! Now slow down. Stop. Slowly lower your legs. Release hands and bring your arms back to your sides. Close your eyes and relax.

6 Make a circle. Sit down on the floor with your feet together in the center and your knees raised. Put your hands on your neighbors' shoulders. Then lean back and lie down. Now lift your legs straight up; then spread them apart so your legs cross your neighbors' legs. Bring your legs back together. Now lower them slowly.

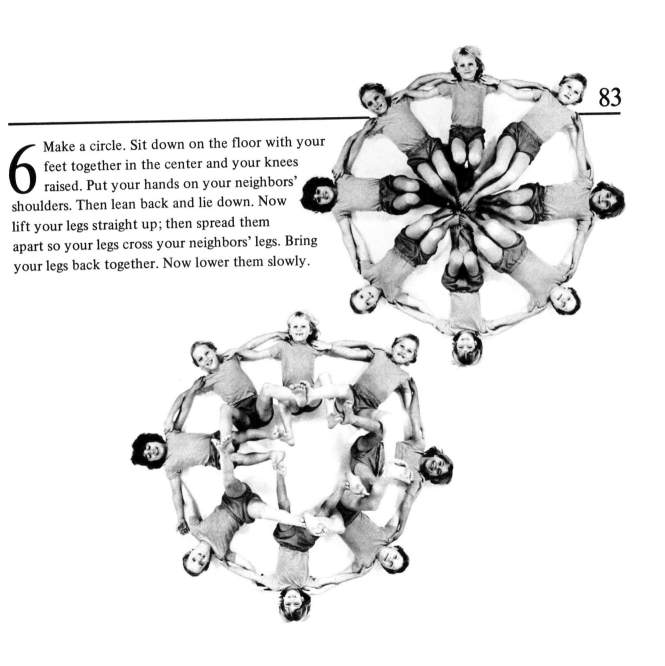

7 Make a circle and lie down on your back. Lift your right leg, wrap your arms around it, and press it toward your stomach. Bring your forehead up to touch your knee. This is the Wind-Releasing Pose (page 41). Lower right leg to the floor and do the same with left leg. Lower left leg. Now lift both legs together and

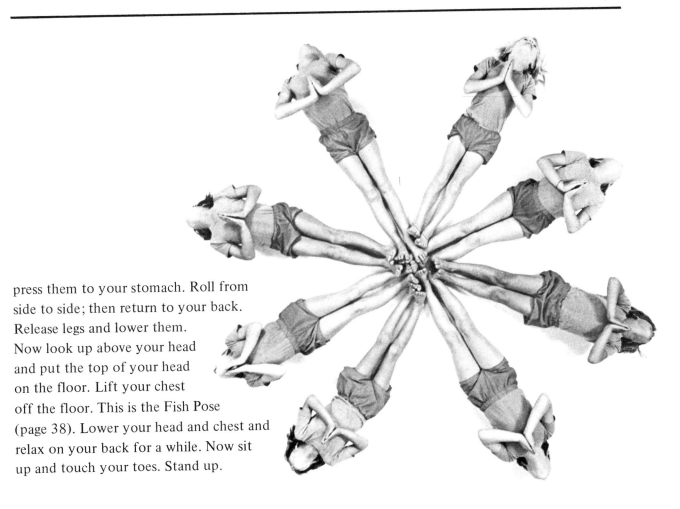

press them to your stomach. Roll from side to side; then return to your back. Release legs and lower them. Now look up above your head and put the top of your head on the floor. Lift your chest off the floor. This is the Fish Pose (page 38). Lower your head and chest and relax on your back for a while. Now sit up and touch your toes. Stand up.

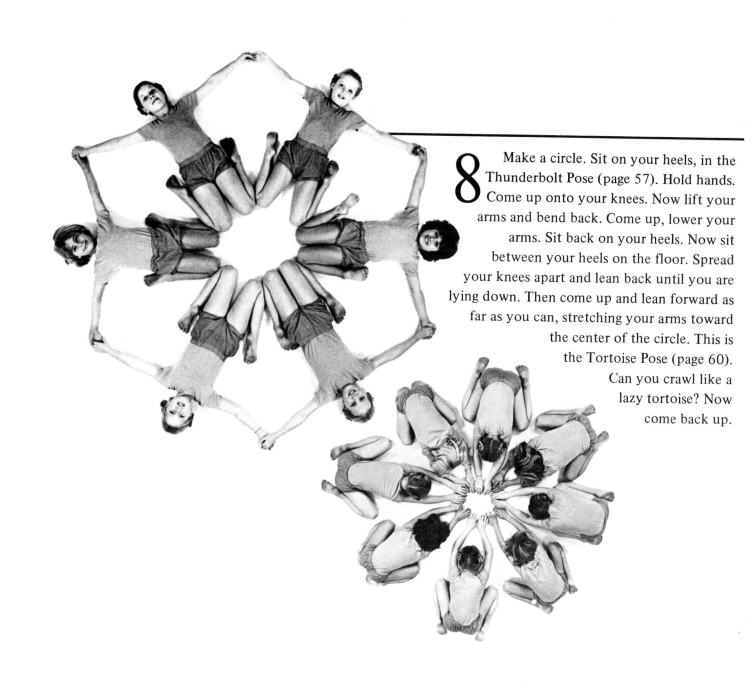

8 Make a circle. Sit on your heels, in the Thunderbolt Pose (page 57). Hold hands. Come up onto your knees. Now lift your arms and bend back. Come up, lower your arms. Sit back on your heels. Now sit between your heels on the floor. Spread your knees apart and lean back until you are lying down. Then come up and lean forward as far as you can, stretching your arms toward the center of the circle. This is the Tortoise Pose (page 60). Can you crawl like a lazy tortoise? Now come back up.

9 Make a circle, kneeling on your knees. Do the Deer Pose (page 58). Your hands are your antlers. Move your head and antlers up and down, and from side to side, as a deer moves while searching for some leaves to eat.

10 Make a circle, kneeling on your knees. Bend forward and stand on "all fours" like a cat. Now inhale with a hissing sound through your mouth while you lower your head and arch your back up like an angry cat. Press your chin to your chest. Exhale through your nose as you raise your head and push your stomach toward the floor. Do the Cat Pose movement four times. Can you meow?

11 Now from a small cat change into a huge kind of cat—a lion. Sit on your crossed heels with your knees apart. Put your hands on your knees with fingers stretched out like claws. Roll your eyes up, extend your tongue, and roar as loud as you can, like a fierce lion. Can you roar louder?

12 Be dwarves. Balance on your knees, grabbing your feet behind you with your hands. Can you walk? Have a dwarf-walk race. Come back into a circle and rest in the Baby Pose (page 62) for a while. Pretend you are a sleeping baby, calm and quiet. Now come up, sitting on your heels. Stand up.

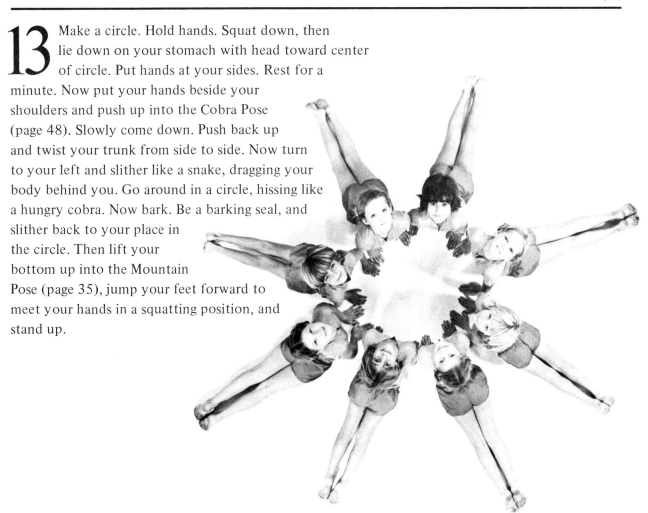

13 Make a circle. Hold hands. Squat down, then lie down on your stomach with head toward center of circle. Put hands at your sides. Rest for a minute. Now put your hands beside your shoulders and push up into the Cobra Pose (page 48). Slowly come down. Push back up and twist your trunk from side to side. Now turn to your left and slither like a snake, dragging your body behind you. Go around in a circle, hissing like a hungry cobra. Now bark. Be a barking seal, and slither back to your place in the circle. Then lift your bottom up into the Mountain Pose (page 35), jump your feet forward to meet your hands in a squatting position, and stand up.

14

Do the Sparrow Pose (page 21). Hop around, searching for food like a little sparrow. Do the Ghost Pose (page 67). Now walk. Don't bump into another ghost! Do the Crab Pose. Stand with your feet apart; then squat down and put your arms between your legs with your palms flat on the floor on the outside of your feet. Straighten arms and lift your body up, pointing toes forward. You can walk like a crab: move both feet to the right and set them down, then pick up hands and move them to the right beside your feet. Keep practicing this and you can walk sideways like a crab. Have a crab-walk race.

15 Do the Lizard Pose.
This pose is like a push-up position,
balancing on your toes and hands. Keep your
body straight. Now try to hop on your hands and
toes, keeping your body straight.

16 Make a circle, holding hands. Sit down and release hands. You are going to be a flower. Put your arms between your legs and under your raised knees. Then lift up your feet and balance in the Flower Pose (page 70). Can you hold your neighbors' hands and balance? What happens to a flower at night? Pretend it's dark and the flower closes up. Lower your head and bring your hands and knees in. Now the sun rises and the flower opens up again. Smile to see the sun. Close the flower again. Then open up, blooming more and more. Stretch your legs out in front, hold hands, and slowly lie down on your back. Release hands; keep them by your sides. Roll your head slightly to one side and relax your whole body. Imagine you are floating high in the sky on a cloud.

17 Have one person lie down on his/her back. The next person lies down with his head resting on first person's stomach and body outstretched perpendicular to the first person. A third person lies down parallel to the first person, resting his head on the second person's stomach. Continue this pattern until all are lying down. Now everybody laugh. Doesn't it feel funny?

Double-Headed Dragon

For this sequence you need two people, one Big and
one Little. Big lifts Little up and Little locks his
ankles around Big's waist. Now Little bends back
and grabs Big's ankles. Big bends forward, putting hands
on the floor. Now Little straightens arms and arches
up as Big walks forward on hands and feet.
Roaring, fire-breathing, etc., optional.

Love
of a Lotus

A lotus is a special flower that stands for love. This song about a lotus can be sung and acted out at the same time using hand positions called *mudras.* Mudras are a way of dancing with your hands. Baba Hari Dass wrote this poem with the mudras and Shankar Heinrich added the music.

THE LO–TUS BLOOMS IN THE WA–TER TO SEE THE SUN'S FACE. THE

SUN TAKES A-ROUND,   AND THE   LO-TUS TURNS IN PACE.   THE

LO-TUS BLOOMS IN THE   WA-TER   TO SHOW LOVE TO THE SUN.   THEY

TALK WITH THEIR EYES, THE LO–TUS CHA–SES FOR FUN. THE

LO–TUS BLOOMS IN THE WA–TER, THE LO–TUS FADES A–WAY.

LOVE IS SHOWN BY THE HEART, NOT BY THE WORDS YOU SAY.

LOVE IS SHOWN BY THE HEART, NOT BY THE WORDS YOU SAY. THE

LO–TUS BLOOMS IN THE WA–TER. STARS TWIN–KLE IN THE SKY.

AN–I–MALS DANCE IN JUN–GLES. THE BIRDS SING WHEN THEY FLY.

Deep Relaxation

TO BE USED at the end of asana practice in the Rest Pose—Shavasana.

Lie down on your back and be comfortable. Close your eyes.

Move your feet up, down, and sideways. Become aware of your feet and how they feel.

Raise your knees off the floor one at a time, and lower them. Do this several times.

Shake your legs a few times. Now your legs are warm, as if covered by a soft warm quilt.

Make tight fists with your hands and release them. Now your hands are getting warm. Feel their warmth.

Imagine that the quilt is covering you up to your neck. It is a comforting feeling—warm and relaxing. The soles of your feet, your knees, thighs, abdomen, and chest all are warm.

You are warm and very relaxed. Your arm muscles, wrists, and palms are warm and relaxed. Your whole body, from your toes to the top of your head, is so relaxed that you don't want to move.

Now go deep into relaxation for fifteen minutes. When you wake up you will not feel tired; you will be alert and refreshed.

Open your eyes and chant Om.

Sit up and stretch your body. Now you are ready for work or play.

Glossary

asana *(ah·suh·nuh):* body posture.

bandha *(buhn·dhuh):* body lock which increases prana.

mudra *(moo·drah):* hand position used to tell stories in
Indian dance. Also it is used to develop concentration.

prana *(prahn):* the universal energy, manifest in
the body mainly through the breath.

pranayama *(prahn·ah·yahm):* deep breathing exercises,
designed to control and direct prana.

AUTHOR BABA HARI DASS receives no money from the sale of his books; his publications are dedicated instead to the needy and homeless children of India. In 1984, in a small village near the Himalayan foothills, he founded Shri Ram Orphanage, with the hope of providing at least some of India's homeless children with a better life. At first there were only 2 children, but within a year 13 had come; then the earthquake in 1991 brought 19 more, and we suddenly became a very large family.

At present writing (1993), our school building is completed and plans are underway for a large dining hall/kitchen facility to better serve the growing needs. With the support and help of many friends and donors, we feel fortunate to be able to make this small but significant difference. For more information about the Orphanage project please feel free to write to us.

Shri Ram Orphanage

Uma Acacia Jones · Suresh Noah Diffenbaugh
Usha Joti Kilpatrick · Sekhar Demian Lee · Manoja Auston Kilpatrick · Bodhi Raymond
Aruna Celeste Hinkle · Chandra Kira Winterbotham · Anandi Heinrich · Sky Rajesh Westerberg
Lalita Lara Kilpatrick